STANDING WAVE

JOHN TAGGART

STANDING WAVE

LOST ROADS PUBLISHERS
NUMBER 38   PROVIDENCE   1993

Some of these poems appeared in the following magazines:
Athena Incognito, Black Warrior Review, Caliban, Conjunctions,
Epoch, Five Fingers Review, Hodos, New American Writing,
Notus: New Writing, Room, Screens & Tasted Parallels, Sulfur,
Temblor, Tyuonyi.

Library of Congress Cataloging in Publication Data

Library of Congress

Taggart, John
    Standing wave
    ISBN 0-918786-43-6
    92-0954569   1993
                        cip

© 1993 by John Taggart; all rights reserved
Published by Lost Roads Publishers
PO Box 5848 Providence, RI 02903
First printing by McNaughton and Gunn
Book design by CD Wright and Forrest Gander
Text design and typesetting by Issa Clubb
Cover art by Sarah Taggart
Special thanks to Anne and Stan Rice, and Kate Abbe, for
helping to make this publication possible.

Contents

LAST TRAIN

Will the last train never come? — Robert Duncan

In and at home in and at home and alone in a room
the space of a room that once was an upstairs bedroom
there is some ambiguity about the space of the room
the room in relation to the page some ambiguity
some in and at home and alone with the idling train
alone with the rising and falling just around the bend
rising and falling and hissing of the idling train
idling just around the bend in the space of the room
there is some ambiguity some but not enough ambiguity
in the space of the room idling just around the bend
the idling train rising and falling and hissing
just around the bend alone with the rising and falling
alone with the idling train in and at home and alone
some ambiguity in relation to the page and the room
about the space of the room there is some ambiguity
upstairs bedroom the space of a room that was a bedroom
in that room in and at home in and at home and alone.

At the top of the stairs the closed door.

One light one headlight in broad daylight
twin sealed-beam headlight on bright
headlight bright and brighter light
headlight bright and brighter than daylight
bright and brighter just around the bend
just around the bend through the trees
through the trees in the space of the room.

Outside the door there could be a garden
there could be a garden of flowers
mingled scent of a garden of flowers.

Three Words From Thomas Bernhard

Of or for of the of the hearing of the hearing of hearing of the ear
or for or for the or for the hearing or for the hearing of
for the hearing of the ear the hearing of the ear is the object
I have written that you have to hear you have to you have to hear
have written that you have to give you have to you have to give ear
written that you who have ears to hear that you have to give ear
for the hearing of the ear the hearing of the ear is the object
or for or for the or for the hearing or for the hearing of
of or for of the of the hearing of the hearing of hearing of the ear
rumbling on the ground a rumbling within itself on the ground
the hearing of the ear is the object for the hearing of the ear
or for the hearing of or for the hearing or for the or for
hearing of the ear of the hearing of the hearing of of or for
you have to hear you have to I have written that you have to hear
you have to give ear you have to have written that you have to give
that you have to give ear written that you who have ears to hear
hearing of the ear of the hearing of the hearing of of or for
or for the hearing of or for the hearing or for the or for
the hearing of the ear is the object for the hearing of the ear.

The night was dark and without the father dark night and no father
no father was there dark night and without the father no father
no father was there dark night in which the little boy cried
the night was dark and without and the little boy began to cry
the little boy cried speak cried speak father to your little boy
the little boy cried speak father to your little boy or else
the little boy cried there was a rumbling there was a sudden flash
, rumbling a rumbling within itself like the roar of an animal
roar of an animal with a golden mane flash of the animal's mane
roar of an animal kiss of an animal with its rough tongue
the animal kisses and wounds the little boy with its rough tongue.

The little boy tries to become smaller smallest in size or degree
tries to become very small tries to make his ear very small
within his smallness the little boy tries to make his ear very small
within his smallness the ear which hears the ear smallest of all
smallest of all within his smallness the ear cannot be a conduit
the little boy believes that this statement is certainly valid
the little boy tries to become smaller smallest in size or degree
he tries to become very small he tries to make his ear very small.

ALL THE STEPS

1

Those who hear the train they had better worry worry
those who hear they had better worry worry.

2

No disgrace to worry to have the worried life blues
might do some good to be worried in the hour of our need.

3

Run run run away going to run run run away
there are those who think they're going to run away.

4

To hear and to be facing and to be facing what is heard
to hear and to be face to face with what is heard.

5

Run run run away they're going to run run run away
there are those who think they're going to run away from the train.

6

Fort built to protect the community from desert raiders
community thought to protect itself from raiders.

7

Those who hear the train they had better worry worry
better worry worry about a gift of tears.

8

Those who are gathered in the fort had better learn
they had better learn how to cure their wounds.

9

The train with its poison and its tongue
the lurking train with its poison and its tongue.

10

Those who are gathered better learn to be insensitive
learn how to put on a show of being insensitive.

11

Danger of its poison and of its tongue
danger of its poison and of its tongue against our teeth.

12

Had better break the habit the habit of prayer
better let the jokes come back to us when we're at prayer.

13

What really kills me is standing in the need of prayer
standing in a gathering in the need of prayer.

14

Don't if we don't if we don't break the habit
we will be made to climb all the steps of the ladder.

15

Brood over someone else's dream: three-story red tower
beneath the tower the train is always departing.

16

Danger of its tongue for those gathered like a group
gathered like a group of all virgins with their downcast eyes.

17

There is this problem with cutting off the prayer hand
there is this problem with the other hand.

18

How insensitive is how those who hear better be
how insensitive how unmoved and cold they had better be.

19

You can call him you can call him up and ask him
if we had only asked for "Sleep Walk" by Santo & Johnny.

20

Red tower green sky three-story tower against green sky
beneath the tower the train is always departing.

21

Don't break it be made to climb all the steps
we don't break it we'll be made to climb all the steps.

22

Ant on the floor the small ant on the kitchen floor
the small ant anticipates by sound or shadow.

23

Light turns out in the kitchen when somebody pulls on the string
those gathered not able to anticipate the danger.

24

If we had only stayed in the school of the prophets
in the school of the prophets who catch thoughts from words.

25

Ant on the floor the small ant on the kitchen floor
those gathered not able to anticipate the danger.

26

Those who are gathered are fondled and taken by the hand
taken by the hand and made to climb all the steps.

27

Perfectly built fort bound to make the community unhappy
bound to make those in the community unhappy.

28

What really kills me is standing in the need of prayer
I'm standing in the need of jokes that come back.

29

Standing in the need of prayer in a perfectly built fort
bound to make you unhappy bound to make me unhappy.

30

Not broken the habit of prayer not been broken
those who are gathered better learn how to cure their wounds.

THE KING OF EYNAN

Three smaller stones around three large stones
the stones removed the earth sifted through
through to a pavement and its low wall
sifted through to a hearth and another pavement
through to the tomb to the tomb of the king
the king on his back his legs bent out of position
skull of the king propped up on a pillow of stones
the king propped up and facing the snowy peaks.

It's too late too late to sever the king's head
too late to break to tie down his legs
it's too late to stop the voice of the king
there are too many tapes of the voice of the king
dub after dub of the master tape
bootlegs and dub after dub of the master tape
too late to break to tie down his legs
it's too late to stop the voice of the king.

BLUEWEED

Valuable (aesthetic point of view)
hides the dark beside the tracks
hides the dark excrement
cinders and fine black soil
the tracks hidden from the road.

The virgins walk in the morning
pick the blueweed flowers
put the flowers in their long hair
fiery blue with pinkish buds
fiery blue with protruding red horns.

I meet the virgins in the morning
the virgins are become sirens
I meet sirens on the road
blueweed flowers in their long hair
fiery blue with pink and red.

STAR DUST

There can be a little consolation in a song
there can be some in the words in a song
inexplicable words come back to me
the words in a song against the sound in my ears
pure and bitter sound in my ears
pure and bitter sound like brushes on a snare
air leaking from a mouthpiece and brushes on a snare.

All there is for me the consolation there can be
there can be consolation there can be some
there is a temptation there is an inclination
an inclination to say there can be none
my inclination to say there can be none
another inclination to say there must be none
there can be a little consolation there can be some.

Mine not necessarily all mine not mine all mine
mine all mine not alone not necessarily mine alone
not mine alone no mine as all there is for me
all there is for me not all that there can be
there can be tea there can be tea for you
all there is for me all there can be
all there is for me not tea not your sympathy.

In The Sense Of

She kept asking why had she been forsaken
why in a narrow room in a narrow bed
narrow bed with twisted sheets
why in the sense of for what purpose
twisted sheets narrow bed
in a narrow bed in a narrow room
why had she been why had she been forsaken.

The vibration there is the vibration the vibration of a fan
there is the vibration there is the continuous vibration
there is the continuous the continuous dull vibration
continuous vibration of a fan small fan on the wooden floor
the vibration the continuous the dull vibration
there is the continuous vibration there is the vibration
the vibration of a fan the vibration there is the vibration
there is the vibration the vibration on the wooden floor
vibration on the floor in the midst of stifling heat
there is the continuous vibration in the heat
continuous vibration of a fan on the floor of a narrow room
in stifling heat there is the continuous vibration
in the midst of stifling heat the vibration on the floor
the vibration on the wooden floor there is the vibration
there is the vibration on the floor of a narrow room
on the floor of a room under the high ceiling of a room
the continuous vibration in a narrow narrow room
continuous vibration continuous vibration beside a narrow bed
narrow narrow room continuous vibration in the room
there is the vibration on the floor under the high ceiling
on the floor of a narrow room there is the vibration of a fan.

She kept asking why had she been forsaken
why in a narrow room in a narrow bed
narrow bed with twisted sheets
why in the sense of for what purpose

The vibration of a fan there is the vibration the vibration
there is the continuous vibration there is the vibration
the continuous dull vibration there is the continuous
small fan on the wooden floor continuous vibration of a fan
the continuous the dull vibration the vibration
there is the vibration there is the continuous vibration
there is the vibration the vibration the vibration of a fan
the vibration on the wooden floor there is the vibration
in the midst of stifling heat vibration on the floor
in the heat there is the continuous vibration
on the floor of a narrow room continuous vibration of a fan
there is the continuous vibration in stifling heat
the vibration on the floor in the midst of stifling heat
there is the vibration the vibration on the wooden floor
on the floor of a narrow room there is the vibration
under the high ceiling of a room on the floor of a room
in a narrow narrow room the continuous vibration
continuous vibration beside a narrow bed continuous vibration
continuous vibration in the room narrow narrow room
on the floor under the high ceiling there is the vibration
there is the vibration of a fan on the floor of a narrow room.

She kept asking why had she been forsaken
why in a narrow room in a narrow bed
narrow bed with twisted sheets
why in the sense of for what purpose
twisted sheets narrow bed

On the floor of a narrow room there is the vibration of a fan
there is the vibration on the floor under the high ceiling
narrow narrow room continuous vibration in the room
continuous vibration continuous vibration beside a narrow bed
the continuous vibration in a narrow narrow room
on the floor of a room under the high ceiling of a room
there is the vibration on the floor of a narrow room
the vibration on the wooden floor there is the vibration
in the midst of stifling heat the vibration on the floor
in stifling heat there is the continuous vibration
continuous vibration of a fan on the floor of a narrow room
there is the continuous vibration in the heat
vibration on the floor in the midst of stifling heat
there is the vibration the vibration on the wooden floor
the vibration of a fan the vibration there is the vibration
there is the continuous vibration there is the vibration
the vibration the continuous the dull vibration
continuous vibration of a fan small fan on the wooden floor
there is the continuous the continuous dull vibration
there is the vibration there is the continuous vibration
the vibration there is the vibration the vibration of a fan.

in a narrow bed in a narrow room
why had she been why had she been forsaken.

There is the vibration of a fan on the floor of a narrow room
on the floor under the high ceiling there is the vibration
continuous vibration in the room narrow narrow room
continuous vibration beside a narrow bed continuous vibration
in a narrow narrow room the continuous vibration
under the high ceiling of a room on the floor of a room
on the floor of a narrow room there is the vibration
there is the vibration the vibration on the wooden floor
the vibration on the floor in the midst of stifling heat
there is the continuous vibration in stifling heat
on the floor of a narrow room continuous vibration of a fan
in the heat there is the continuous vibration
in the midst of stifling heat vibration on the floor
the vibration on the wooden floor there is the vibration
there is the vibration the vibration the vibration of a fan
there is the vibration there is the continuous vibration
the continuous the dull vibration the vibration
small fan on the wooden floor continuous vibration of a fan
the continuous dull vibration there is the continuous
there is the continuous vibration there is the vibration
the vibration of a fan there is the vibration the vibration.

BLACK AND WHITE CLOSE-UP

1

Close-up black and white close-up of corn stalks
no trees at the end no dirt road on the right
tracks near the dirt road not to be seen
the end of the field not to be seen
not to be seen in the black and white close-up
only corn stalks only so many corn stalks
so many bleached and flattened out corn stalks
I had not thought there could be so many
so many bones and whispy bits of hair
whispy bits of hair of those who have been taken.

2

Sand on black and white close-up of corn stalks
some fine sand sprinkled on the close-up
fine sand held in the cupped hand and sprinkled
fine sand of a yellowish-red color
yellowish-red on the black and white close-up
on the corn stalks so many corn stalks
so many bleached and flattened out corn stalks
I had not thought there could be so many
so many bones and whispy bits of hair
whispy bits of hair of those who have been taken.

3

Sand on black and white close-up of corn stalks
some fine sand sprinkled on the close-up
fine sand held in the cupped hand and sprinkled
fine sand of a yellowish-red color
yellowish-red on the black and white close-up
on the corn stalks so many corn stalks
yellowish-red sand on each of the many corn stalks
sand sprinkled on each of the many corn stalks
on the many bones and whispy bits of hair
whispy bits of hair of those who have been taken.

4

Sand on black and white close-up of corn stalks
some fine sand sprinkled on the close-up
fine sand held in the cupped hand and sprinkled
fine sand of a yellowish-red color
yellowish-red on the black and white close-up
the sand keeps shifting so many corn stalks
the sand can't cover each of the many corn stalks
the sand is sprinkled the sand keeps shifting
so many bones and whispy bits of hair
whispy bits of hair of those who have been taken.

5

Close-up black and white close-up of corn stalks
no trees at the end no dirt road on the right
tracks near the dirt road not to be seen
the end of the field not to be seen
not to be seen in the black and white close-up
only corn stalks only so many corn stalks
so many bleached and flattened out corn stalks
I had not thought there could be so many
so many bones and whispy bits of hair
whispy bits of hair of those who have been taken.

6

White on black and white close-up of corn stalks
white India ink drawn on the close-up
cross-hatched lines drawn this way and that
cross-hatched lines of white ink
white India ink on the black and white close-up
on the corn stalks so many corn stalks
so many bleached and flattened out corn stalks
I had not thought there could be so many
so many bones and whispy bits of hair
whispy bits of hair of those who have been taken.

7

White on black and white close-up of corn stalks
white India ink drawn on the close-up
cross-hatched lines drawn this way and that
cross-hatched lines of white ink
white India ink on the black and white close-up
on the corn stalks so many corn stalks
white India ink on each of the many corn stalks
cross-hatched lines on each of the many corn stalks
on the many bones and whispy bits of hair
whispy bits of hair of those who have been taken.

White on black and white close-up of corn stalks
white India ink drawn on the close-up
cross-hatched lines drawn this way and that
cross-hatched lines of white ink
white India ink on the black and white close-up
corn stalks still visible between cross-hatched lines
the lines can't cover each of the many corn stalks
the lines are drawn the lines can't cover
so many bones and whispy bits of hair
whispy bits of hair of those who have been taken.

9

Close-up black and white close-up of corn stalks
no trees at the end no dirt road on the right
tracks near the dirt road not to be seen
the end of the field not to be seen
not to be seen in the black and white close-up
only corn stalks only so many corn stalks
so many bleached and flattened out corn stalks
I had not thought there could be so many
so many bones and whispy bits of hair
whispy bits of hair of those who have been taken.

10

Black and white close-up of corn stalks torn in two
black and white close-up torn in two
close-up held by the corners and torn in two
held by and torn held by and torn in two
the black and white close-up torn completely in two
corn stalks torn so many of the corn stalks
so many bleached and flattened out corn stalks
I had not thought there could be so many
so many bones and whispy bits of hair
whispy bits of hair of those who have been taken.

11

Black and white close-up of corn stalks torn in two
black and white close-up torn in two
close-up held by the corners and torn in two
held by and torn held by and torn in two
the black and white close-up torn completely in two
corn stalks torn so many of the corn stalks
so many of the bleached and flattened out corn stalks
each of the many corn stalks torn in two
the many bones and bits of hair torn in two
whispy bits of hair of those who have been taken.

12

Black and white close-up of corn stalks torn in two
black and white close-up torn in two
close-up held by the corners and torn in two
held by and torn held by and torn in two
the black and white close-up torn completely in two
corn stalks torn so many of the corn stalks
so many of the bleached and flattened out corn stalks
each of the stalks torn completely in two
bones and bits of hair torn completely in two
whispy bits of hair of those who have been taken.

In And Under

Bent over a pianist an attentive reader
bent over almost a mournful figure
she wishes to untie the knot
she has set her heart on untying the knot.

Her fingers move in the motion of combs
she has made her fingers into combs
motion in and under the weaves
in and under all the transparent weaves.

She has set her heart on untying the knot
she wishes to untie the central knot
could be the head of an animal
the head of an animal under the weaves.

In and under her fingers come upon a cube
nothing to grasp or to kiss
a cube full of immense and empty space
her fingers move in immense and empty space.

QUESTION NO QUESTION

Question no question: shall they gather at the river
crystal river where the children are held under
question no question for the river brethren
they will gather with the children in the river.

If you go out in a glass-bottomed boat on the river
you can see the children under the crystal river
question no question for the river brethren
they will gather with the children in the river.

The robes of the children are tattered and torn
they have lost their crowns in the river
question no question for the river brethren
they will gather with the children in the river.

The children float on the bottom of the shining river
dead leaves on the bottom of the river
question no question for the river brethren
they will gather with the children in the river.

THE FACE OF LOVE

Hard to be face to face
to be and to stay
to stay face to face
with the face of love.

Eve closed her eyes
(Blake's notebook)
when the forcing serpent
when the serpent came.

Hard to be face to face
to be and to stay
stay between the tracks
when the snake train comes.

Snake with its poison
its poison its tongue
its bright eyes
bright and brighter eyes.

How Long

1

The word to the action to the action of being hit
the word to the action the word one word
the word one word not enough one not enough
not enough one not enough to the action of being hit
enough if the action were a one time action
if the action of being hit were a one time action
the word one word not enough one not enough
not enough one not enough to the action of being hit.

2

The word to the action to the action of being hit
the word one word not enough one not enough
not enough one not enough to the action of being hit
one plus one two words two enough to the action
the action of being hit one a one time action
two words enough to the one one time action
not enough one not enough to the action of being hit
one plus one two words two enough to the action.

Marked moderato
not moderato
largo

largo
largo as can be
as largo as can be.

4

The word to the action to the action of being hit
the word one word not enough one not enough
not enough one not enough to the action of being hit
one plus one two words combination of two words
combination of two words two one-syllable words
two one-syllable words to the action
not enough one not enough to the action of being hit
one plus one two words combination of two words.

TAKE AWAY

Little hand the shadow of a hand on the surface of the moon
little hand taken away in the game of take away
little hand taken away the shadow of a little hand.

Unloosened left unloosened as from cloud cover left exposed
left unloosened and exposed a pale and gleaming surface
paler and more gleaming than the moon at Tours
paler and more gleaming and more perfectly a sphere
and more and more than the moon at Tours or the moon at Amboise
on the more and more surface a less pale a darker area
only slightly darker ivory and the shadow of a hand on ivory
a slightly darker area with the shape of a wedge
the shape of a wedge and the shadow of a hand
a slightly darker area and the shadow of a different hand
at the center of the slightly darker wedge-shaped area
at the center of the area another darker area
another slightly darker area another slightly darker still
slightly darker still one shadow and another shadow
one shadow one and another shadow of a different hand.

Simple rule simple condition of the game with a little hand
simple rule simple condition of the game of take away
simple rule simple condition the rule of my turn then his turn
little hand the shadow of a hand on the surface of the moon
little hand taken away the shadow of a little hand
the shape of a wedge and the shadow of a hand
slightly darker area and the shadow of a different hand.

STANDING WAVE

1

Line to line connection of line to line with line to line
one line to line with one line to line at a time
connection of one line to line with one line to line
I connect one line to line with one line to line
connection of one line to line with one line to line at a time
within one line to line a room within one line to line
connection of one line to line with one line to line
one line to line with one line to line at a time
line to line connection of line to line with line to line
there is a standing wave so high in the middle of my room
the folds of the wave in perfect obedience
standing wave so high in the middle of my room
folds upon folds of the wave in perfect obedience
there is a standing wave so high I can't get over it
line to line connection of line to line with line to line
one line to line with one line to line at a time
connection of one line to line with one line to line
within one line to line a room within one line to line
connection of one line to line with one line to line at a time
I connect one line to line with one line to line
connection of one line to line with one line to line
one line to line with one line to line at a time
line to line connection of line to line with line to line.

2

Line to line with line to line connection of line to line
one line to line at a time with one line to line
line to line with one line to line connection of one
line to line with one line to line I connect one
line to line with one line to line at a time connection of one
within one line to line a room within one line to line
line to line with one line to line connection of one
one line to line at a time with one line to line
line to line with line to line connection of line to line
there is a standing wave soo-oo-o-oo high in the middle
foo-oo-o-oolds of wave in perfect obedience
standing wave soo-oo-o-oo high in the middle of my room
foo-oo-o-oolds upon foo-oo-o-oolds of the wave
standing wave soo-oo-o-oo high I can't get over it
line to line with line to line connection of line to line
one line to line at a time with one line to line
line to line with one line to line connection of one
within one line to line a room within one line to line
line to line with one line to line at a time connection of one
line to line with one line to line I connect one
line to line with one line to line connection of one
one line to line at a time with one line to line
line to line with line to line connection of line to line.

3

Line to line disconnection of one line from line to line
line to line disconnection of one line to line
disconnection of one line to line from line to line
one line to line from two of the other line to line
one from two of the other to make an opening
I disconnect one line to line to make an opening in my room
disconnection of one line to line from line to line
line to line disconnection of one line to line
line to line disconnection of one line from line to line
there was a standing wave so wide in the middle of my room
the folds of the wave in perfect obedience
standing wave so wide in the middle of my room
folds upon folds of the wave in perfect obedience
there was a standing wave so wide I couldn't get around it
line to line disconnection of one line from line to line
line to line disconnection of one line to line
disconnection of one line to line from line to line
I disconnect one line to line to make an opening in my room
one from two of the other to make an opening
one line to line from two of the other line to line
disconnection of one line to line from line to line
line to line disconnection of one line to line
line to line disconnection of one line from line to line.

4

One line from line to line disconnection of line to line
one line to line disconnection of line to line
line to line from line to line disconnection of one
the other line to line one line to line from two
to make an opening one from two of the other
to make an opening in my room I disconnect one line to line
line to line from line to line disconnection of one
one line to line disconnection of line to line
one line from line to line disconnection of line to line
there was a standing wave soo-oo-o-oo wide in the middle
foo-oo-o-oolds of the wave in perfect obedience
standing wave soo-oo-o-oo wide in the middle of my room
foo-oo-o-oolds upon foo-oo-o-oolds of the wave
standing wave soo-oo-o-oo wide I couldn't get around it
one line from line to line disconnection of line to line
one line to line disconnection of line to line
line to line from line to line disconnection of one
to make an opening in my room I disconnect one line to line
to make an opening one from two of the other
the other line to line one line to line from two
line to line from line to line disconnection of one
one line to line disconnection of line to line
one line from line to line disconnection of line to line.

5

Line to line demarcation of line to line from line to line
demarcation of three line to line from line to line
three from line to line from other line to line
demarcation from other line to line by being made darker
three line to line demarcation of three by being made darker
I make three darker to make an opening in my room
three from line to line from other line to line
demarcation of three line to line from line to line
line to line demarcation of line to line from line to line
there will be a standing wave so deep in the middle of my room
the folds of the wave in perfect obedience
standing wave so deep in the middle of my room
folds upon folds of the wave in perfect obedience
there will be a standing wave so deep I won't get under it
line to line demarcation of line to line from line to line
demarcation of three line to line from line to line
three from line to line from other line to line
I make three darker to make an opening in my room
three line to line demarcation of three by being made darker
demarcation from other line to line by being made darker
three from line to line from other line to line
demarcation of three line to line from line to line
line to line demarcation of line to line from line to line.

Line to line from line to line demarcation of line to line
line to line from line to line demarcation of three
line to line from other line to line from three
being made darker demarcation from other line to line
demarcation of three by being made darker three line to line
to make an opening in my room I make three darker
line to line from other line to line from three
line to line from line to line demarcation of three
line to line from line to line demarcation of line to line
there will be a standing wave soo-oo-o-oo deep in the middle
foo-oo-o-oolds of the wave in perfect obedience
standing wave soo-oo-o-oo deep in the middle of my room
foo-oo-o-oolds upon foo-oo-o-oolds of the wave
there'll be a standing wave soo-oo-o-oo deep I won't get under it
line to line from line to line demarcation of line to line
line to line from line to line demarcation of three
line to line from other line to line from three
to make an opening in my room I make three darker
demarcation of three by being made darker three line to line
being made darker demarcation from other line to line
line to line from other line to line from three
line to line from line to line demarcation of three
line to line from line to line demarcation of line to line.

FREE GIFTS

Before the kiss there are gifts there are free gifts
members of the studio audience receive free gifts
each member receives a string of blossoms
each member of the audience asked to bend down
string of plastic apple blossoms placed around each neck
before the kiss there are gifts there are free gifts
members of the studio audience receive free gifts
each member receives a "night with the stars"
each member photographed with blossoms around each neck
polaroid photograph pinned to "night with the stars" curtain
roar of an animal with golden mane flash of its mane
roar of an animal with its mane kiss of an animal
sudden kiss of an animal with its rough tongue
sudden kiss for each member of the audience
sudden kiss sudden wound for each member of the audience
before the kiss there are gifts there are free gifts
members of the studio audience receive free gifts
each member receives a string of blossoms
each member photographed with blossoms around each neck
polaroid photograph pinned to "night with the stars" curtain.

ALTERNATE TAKE

The sound in my ears against the words in a song
this pure and bitter sound in my ears
pure and bitter sound like brushes on a snare
air leaking from a mouthpiece and brushes on a snare
this pure and bitter sound like sandpaper
sandpaper rubbing against the words in a song
sandpaper rubbing against the consolation in a song.

All there is for me the consolation there can be
the consolation there can be in a song
sandpaper rubbing against the consolation
sandpaper rubbing against a little consolation
sandpaper rubbing against some of the consolation
this is not a matter of my inclination
this is not a matter of my or your inclination.

Mine all mine not alone not necessarily mine alone
not mine alone a little for you and some for me
there can be a little consolation for you
there can be some consolation for me
this pure and bitter sound like sandpaper
sandpaper rubbing against all that there can be.

REREADING

1

He has closed the door to his room and he is reading
he has closed the door and he is reading a poem
he is reading a poem he is rereading one of his own poems
it is one of his own poems a poem about singing
it is a poem about singing about reasons for singing
reasons one of the reasons for singing
the reason was to light the most quiet light
the reason was to light the light that was radiantia
radiantia that was a singing light in darkness.

Light through the window rectangles of morning light
light through the window a rectangle on the floor
rectangle of dragon morning light on the floor
it is like a carpet like a tawny dragon carpet on the floor
the carpet does not transport him to a radiant realm
he does not cry out to be transported to a radiant realm
light through the window rectangle on the wall
rectangle of morning light on the wall
it is like a screen on which only light is projected.

2

He has closed the door to his room and he is reading
he has closed the door and he is reading a poem
he is reading a poem he is rereading one of his own poems
it is one of his own poems a poem about singing
it is another poem about singing about the reasons for singing
one of the reasons another one of the reasons for singing
the reason was to lift up bones in light
to lift up bones in curled leaves and petals
in a shining ring that is an ardor and a blossoming.

Light through the window rectangles of morning light
light through the window a rectangle on the floor
a rectangle of morning light on the wall
it is not the light in which the bones were to be lifted up
the bones in curled leaves and petals
in which the bones were to be a shining ring
he had intended the greatest gifts
his intention had been rebuked
his intention of the greatest gifts rebuked and scorned.

3

He has closed the door to his room and he is reading
he has closed the door and he is reading a poem
he is reading a poem he is rereading one of his own poems
it is one of his own poems a poem about singing
it is another poem about singing about the reasons for singing
yet another reason related to the other reasons
the reason was to sing for heart's ease
to sing with the singing bones for heart's ease in a ring
away from all light to sing in a ring in true night.

Light through the window rectangles of morning light
light through the window on the floor on the wall
rectangles of morning light carpet and screen
it is not the light in which the bones were to be lifted up
not the light in which the bones were a shining ring
he does not cry out to be lifted up in a ring
he had turned away from the highway
he had turned away from reflecting signs
he had not turned away from all light not all light.

4

He has closed the door to his room and he is reading
he has closed the door and he is reading a poem
he is reading a poem he is rereading one of his own poems
it is one of his own it's a poem about crossing
about crossing a desert of glass to the crystal
another reason related to other reasons
another reason child on fire napalmed child
the child is in the crystal the central crystal
central crystal the fire-lit crystal of the wilderness.

Light through the window rectangles of morning light
light through the window on the floor on the wall
rectangles of morning light in which the bones were not a ring
he had been among those who couldn't wait for veiled light
the procession of those who couldn't wait
who crossed to fire-lit crystal of the wilderness
light from fire-lit crystal of the wilderness
all light was in all light was from
he had thought all light was in was from the crystal.

5

He has closed the door to his room and he is reading
he has closed the door and he is reading a poem
he is reading a poem he is rereading one of his own poems
it is one of his own poems about singing
it is a poem about singing about reasons for singing
one of the reasons related to the other reasons
reason was to brighten the corner where you are
not wait to be lit up not wait to embrace child
not wait to shine where you are shed your light afar.

Light through the window rectangles of morning light
light through the window on the floor on the wall
rectangles of almost too bright morning light
he could not wait to be lit up
he could not wait to embrace the child
could not wait to be in a shining ring not one heart alone
he is not in a ring he is alone in his room
the morning light is almost too bright
he's not in a ring he is alone he is one heart alone.

6

He has closed the door to his room and he is reading
he has closed the door and he is reading a poem
he is reading a poem he is rereading one of his own poems
it is one of his own poems about wandering
it is a poem about wandering into a red room red after black
no red goes deeper than red after black
there was a reason for wandering
the reason was screaming from the child of pain
screaming from the child given only one picture.

Light through the window rectangles of morning light
light through the open window wide open window
rectangles of bright morning light
he questions whether this light won't turn into that light
whether this room won't turn into that room
no red goes deeper than red after black
he questions whether he won't be willing to be child
not Vietnamese not Christ the child of pain
he questions whether willing has anything to do with it.

7

He has closed the door to his room and he is reading
he has closed the door and he is reading a poem
he is reading a poem he is rereading one of his own poems
it is one of his own poems about walking
it is a poem about walking about a corridor of rooms
about walking down a corridor of empty rooms
the reason was not his reason
it wasn't his reason the birth was their reason
their reason they had to know how the light was born.

Light through the window rectangles of morning light
light through the wide open window
rectangles of what could turn into crystal light
alone in his room not one of those rooms
not one of the empty rooms on a corridor of empty rooms
he questions whether this room won't turn into that red room
they had to know the secret of the birth
he questions whether his reason was not their reason
he questions whether they are happy in their knowledge.

8

He has closed the door to his room and he is reading
he has closed the door and he is reading a poem
he is reading a poem he is rereading one of his own poems
it is one of his own poems about sitting
it is a poem about the king sitting
about the king about the king sitting alone
the reason was the same reason his reason the same reason
it's the same reason the king was sitting alone
there is no flower and there can be no hope of rest.

Light through the window rectangles of morning light
light through the window that can't be shut
rectangles of what could turn what could return
the king nailed the singer of the voice
the singer was nailed to the wall
no phosphorescent flower in the king's hand
not in a ring alone he is sitting alone
no phosphorescent flower in his hand
there is no flower and there can be no hope of rest.

VAGUELY HARMLESS

1

Harmless to manipulate the already manipulated
vaguely harmless to do what has already been done
to manipulate the black and white close-up
to remanipulate the black and white close-up
vaguely harmless because maybe not so harmless
corn stalks so many corn stalks
so many bleached and flattened out corn stalks
maybe not so harmless to remanipulate the close-up
so many bones and whispy bits of hair
bones and bits of hair stuck in the memory.

2

Forget about sand on black and white close-up
fine-grained sand sprinkled on the close-up
about sand held in the cupped hand and sprinkled
I know something about sand painting
and I know something about sand
sand comes from the whisper of the horn
from the grainy whisper of the horn of the voice
from the grainy whisper of the horn
sand-words come from the whisper
sand-words come from the whisper of the horn.

3

Forget about sand on black and white close-up
fine-grained sand sprinkled on the close-up
I know about holding and sprinkling
and I know something about sand
forget about sand as a medium for forgetting
if so many corn stalks could only be forgotten
sand comes from the whisper of the horn
all the sand of the desert from the whisper
all the sand-words come from the whisper
whisper of the horn circulating over the desert.

4

Forget about sand on black and white close-up
fine-grained sand sprinkled on the close-up
I know something about sand painting
and I know something about sand
sand can't be a medium for forgetting
can't be a medium for forgetting so many bones
sand comes from the whisper of the horn
sand-words come from the whisper of the horn
all the sand-words I thought were my words
come from the grainy whisper over the desert.

5

Harmless to manipulate the already manipulated
vaguely harmless to do what has already been done
to manipulate the black and white close-up
to remanipulate the black and white close-up
vaguely harmless because not so harmless
corn stalks so many corn stalks
so many bleached and flattened out corn stalks
not so harmless to remanipulate the close-up
so many bones and whispy bits of hair
bones and bits of hair stuck in the memory.

6

Forget about snow on black and white close-up
about snow flakes drawn on the close-up
white India ink snow flakes drawn by hand
snow flakes drawn to cover the field completely
I know something about drawing snow flakes
and I know something about snow
snow comes from the whisper of the horn
from the white whisper of the horn of the voice
snow-words come from the whisper
not from Celan from the whisper of the horn.

7

Forget about snow on black and white close-up
about snow flakes drawn on the close-up
I know something about drawing snow flakes
and I know something about snow
forget about snow as a medium for forgetting
if so many corn stalks could only be forgotten
snow comes from the whisper of the horn
all the snow in the field from the whisper
all the snow-words come from the whisper
not Celan from whisper of the horn over the field.

Forget about snow on black and white close-up
about snow flakes drawn on the close-up
I know about drawing with white India ink
and I know something about snow
snow can't be a medium for forgetting
can't be a medium for forgetting so many bones
snow comes from the whisper of the horn
snow-words come from the whisper of the horn
all the snow-words I thought were my words
not Celan from the white whisper over the field.

9

Harmless to manipulate the already manipulated
vaguely harmless to do what has already been done
to manipulate the black and white close-up
to remanipulate the black and white close-up
vaguely harmless because not harmless
corn stalks so many corn stalks
so many bleached and flattened out corn stalks
not harmless to remanipulate the close-up
so many bones and whispy bits of hair
bones and bits of hair stuck in the memory.

10

Forget about wind on black and white close-up
about blow wind blow on the close-up
close-up held for the wind to blow on and to tear
I know something about holding photographs
and I know something about the wind
the wind comes from the whisper of the horn
from the tearing whisper of the horn of the voice
wind-words come from the whisper
wind-words come from the whisper of the horn.

11

Forget about wind on black and white close-up
about blow wind blow on the close-up
I know something about holding photographs
and I know something about the wind
forget about the wind as a medium for forgetting
if so many corn stalks could only be forgotten
the wind comes from the whisper of the horn
all the blow wind blow from the whisper
all the wind-words come from the whisper
from the blow whisper over desert and field.

12

Forget about wind on black and white close-up
about blow wind blow on the close-up
I know about holding photographs by the corners
and I know something about the wind
the wind can't be a medium for forgetting
can't be a medium for forgetting so many bones
the wind comes from the whisper of the horn
wind-words come from the whisper of the horn
all the wind-words I thought were my words
blowing and tearing whisper over desert and field.

MILK AND SEED

Had cried she had cried and cried for it
had known crying was her only resource
what could not be got by work
what could be got only by crying.

What could be got was the mother's milk
milk in response to her crying
milk all over her head and hands
in response flow of the mother's milk.

Had cried she had cried and cried for it
had known crying was her only resource
there was no question of work
no question of ceasing her crying.

What could be got was the father's seed
kneeling with her head bent
kneeling with her hands raised
in response the father's milky seed.

READY OR NOT

1

Ready or not to be included in singing ready or not
to be included in singing "power"
singing "power" with a miked bass drum
first syllable of "power" with a miked bass drum
to be included in singing to stop singing.

2

Ready or not to be included in repeating ready or not
to be included in repeating words
in repeating four words of the prayer
repeating what has been done should have been done
to be included in repeating to stop repeating.

3

Ready or not to be included in gathering ready or not
to be included in gathering together
gathering together with the white women of Delvaux
white women of Delvaux at the train station
to be included in gathering to stop gathering.

LIKE THAT AND THEN

Thought he said "touch me"
she thought he had
thought he'd said that
said that as she turned.

That was what she heard
something like that
it was like that
like that in a garden.

That was what she heard
like that and then
and then the train
sudden train in a garden.

Thought he said "touch me"
thought he had
thought he said that
said that as she turned.

LOUDER

Whisper's getting louder whisper's gradually getting louder
whisper's very gradually getting louder
whisper's very very gradually getting louder.